**By Yon Bonnie**

**By Yon Bonnie** Braes

# For Maurice

# By Yon Bonnie Banks
# By Yon Bonnie Braes

## A Tayside Childhood

## By Vera Milne

First Edition

First published in Great Britain in November 2003
Published by Vera Milne

Vera Milne is identified as the author of this book.

Publisher – Vera Milne 81 Broadmeads, Ware SG12 9HX

Printed in United Kingdom by PDC Copyprint,
147 Station Road, Edgware, Middlesex HA8 7JS

Illustrations © Dawn Brooks

ISBN 0-9546375-0-X

# TABLE OF CONTENTS

# PREFACE

This is an amusing, nostalgic yet moving account of everyday living in a small Scottish town on the bonnie banks and braes of the River Tay just after the Second World War, as remembered by me, Vera Milne.

People from all parts of Scotland will be able to identify with many of the events and happenings.
The book in most parts is written in the vernacular and in the way in which things were spoken.
The first chapter is an armchair tour of Tayport, the town in which I was born and bred. It also reflects on happenings in other tayside towns and cities - Broughty Ferry, Wormit, Newport and Dundee.
I am recalling happenings at that time, between 1946-1956. Mostly happy but inevitably some sad memories.

The following chapters are on a lighter note about life and customs and could relate to Scots anywhere. If they were not alive at that time, then their parents and grandparents no doubt were.
Let's preserve our history and chuckle.

# Acknowledgements

I would like to thank my friends and family for helping me to write this book.

It would be impossible to list everyone but particular mention would be appropriate for my niece Dawn Brooks.
Dawn as the illustrator has captured the feel of the time in which it was written. Her pictures paint a thousand words.

A special thanks go to the following;-
To my friend Jean Dickinson, for proof reading.

To Philip Harrison from Wendling for  designing the Front Cover

To Angus Hill for allowing me to use his photograph of the West Lights on the Front Cover.

# CHAPTER ONE
## (MAP TAYPORT CIRCA 1946-1956)

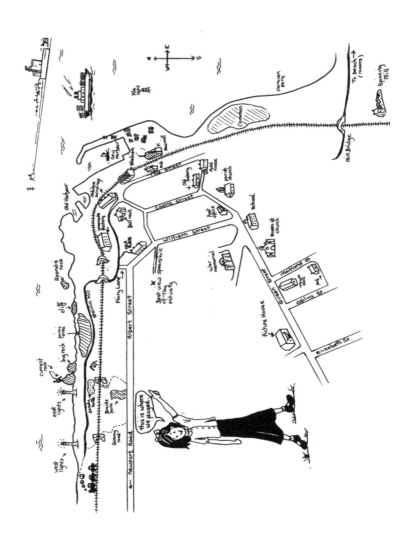

# A Post War Childhood spent primarily on the Banks and Braes of the River Tay

Please reflect with me all you….Tayportonians. Most of the places and events to which I refer will hold memories for you or perhaps memories will be awakened on reading and reminding ourselves of life in the late forties/ early fifties in Tayport.

I was born or should I say the 'aeroplane' landed at 9.45 a.m. on Monday the 15th December at 8 Isla Place Tayport in 1941 , with Dr Mackintosh in attendance, and I was brought up there until I was about 13 years old.
Isla Place was quite unique. It was also known as the Brickies as it was one of the first places to be built in Tayport with bricks. There were 16 houses or flats; we just called them all houses not flats.
In some ways Isla Place was behind the times as we only had gas - no electric- gas lighting too of course. The gas lamp stem was in the middle of the mantelpiece and the mantle was very delicate and easily broken. It was broken many times accidentally and there was no mantle available to replace it so we

had light only from the coal fire. It was very cosy on those occasions as we sat watching the flames go up the lum and listening to stories of long ago…

There were only outside toilets. Three of the houses had to share one toilet.
Newspaper cut in to squares was tied neatly on the cistern for toilet paper.

There was a separate washing house for washing clothes round the back. When you went through the close, the washing house was on the right in the Back Dykes. There was a boiler. When I say boiler, it was a sunken metal tub with a coal fire underneath it. It was very difficult to light. The women had to get up about 5 a.m. to light it as it took a very long time to heat up. There were about four wooden wash tubs on stands. These wash tubs looked just like the wooden tubs you get now from the garden centre. There was a washing day rota and you could only use the washing house on your allocated day.
We also had our own outside coal shed.
These were alongside the wash house.
They are still there today but presumably have another use other than for coal.
From Albert St., the front of Isla Place was

just known as The Front, the coal sheds for these are still there backing on to the pavement. The toilets were beneath the outside stairs; these too were shared by about three different families. This could mean sharing one toilet with about 16 people!

There was quite a community spirit there. (I mean in Isla Place not the toilets!) The housewives used to come out and lean on the wall looking out to Broughty Ferry and discuss the local news and gossip. We could see the Broughty Lifeboat Shed from this wall and on many occasions could see the flares go up from a boat in distress. We then heard very clearly the two loud bangs from the rockets or maroons that went off in Broughty Ferry to call the Lifeboat out to an emergency (it used to be one bang to call the Coastguard out and two to call the Lifeboat out). Where the river Tay meets the North Sea is a very treacherous area indeed, particularly in bad weather for small boats. We could see this area, called the Bar of the Tay from Isla Place so were on the look out in bad weather for any problems in the river. We used to hear the Foghorn blowing repeatedly to warn ships of any danger.
*See location Map at front of book.

It was here in later years, namely on Tuesday December 8th 1959 that the Broughty Ferry Lifeboat disaster occurred when the Lifeboat - The Mona - was called out to just past the Bar of the Tay in a very severe gale to rescue a boat in distress. The particular boat requiring assistance was the North Carr Light Ship; it had broken adrift from her moorings off Fife Ness in the North Sea just past St Andrews and was in dire trouble.
The Light Ship managed to get itself to safe waters, namely St Andrews Bay, independently of the Lifeboat, but sadly there was no more contact with the Lifeboat itself after they radioed that they had cleared the Bar of the Tay (crossing the Bar was expected to be the most difficult part of the trip).
Then there was silence...........the crew never to be heard from again. This was put down as a mystery of the sea.

The Lifeboat was found undamaged except for a broken mast on the Buddon Ness Sands near Carnoustie at daybreak.
The 28 years old coxswain although living in Dundee with his wife and baby daughter Gail, was a Tayport man. His name was Ronald Grant.

It was noted that his daughter was named
Gail and that he died in a Gale.
The entire crew of eight lost their lives.
(We watched this drama unfold from our side
of the river).

All our friends and neighbours were just
watching and staring out to the Estuary
shaking their heads in shocked disbelief.
We could see the Lifeboat Shed at Broughty
Ferry from Isla Place. We were directly
opposite. The Lifeboat Shed doors were red
in colour but when the doors were open, the
inside revealed white or cream on the walls.
We could see this Shed very clearly from the
Back Dykes at Isla Place. When we saw the
white walls, we knew that more than likely
the Lifeboat had been called out. Bearing in
mind the river is almost 3 x miles wide
between Tayport and Broughty Ferry, this
was a very clear view.

# CHAPTER TWO
## (SHIVERY BITE)

# ARMCHAIR TOUR
## (see map at front of chapter one)

Leaving Isla Place, turn left out of the
Close down the brae, then turn left up about
50 yards to what was the first Railway
Bridge* ( excluding foot bridges). This was
situated on the right; on the left of this Bridge
was Fairy Lane. Continuing on another 50
yards there was another Railway Bridge; this
time the Bridge was almost level with the top
of the Big Cliff. The road from the top of the
Cliff running down the hill was, and still is,
called the Stainin Hill. The road continued on
past the Sandy Hole on your left then taking
you to the East and West Lights on your
right. The Lighthouses were more commonly
known as the First and Second Lights.

**Let me relate a typical day for us who had
the good fortune to live in Tayport.**
At the beginning of the braes, just as I said at
the first bridge, there was a large house called
Wellcraig and you could reach a good point
from here to start your day. Each day was
like an adventure.
This was a good place to join the stoney
beach, just to the left of Wellcraig house.
There was what was known as the Roondie

rock. At high tide the Roondie rock was almost like a little island.

The fishermen used to recite the rhyme;-

Roond and roond the Roondie rock<br>
The ragged rascal ran<br>
If you could tell how many R's are in that<br>
You are a very wise man.

They recited this to us when we approached them there. We were convinced that this was where the rhyme was written!

This was a very popular area for fishing. Many of the local men would come here to fish. They always had a good catch from here as when the tide came in it was quite deep and you didn't need to cast out very far.

They used to catch 'Flooks' or Flounders which were delicious to eat. Just as well as we had to eat lots of them!

Going along up river a few yards from there and you came to the beach at the bottom of the Cliff, which is where we found the nicest shells and unusual stones and rocks -we even found razor shells here.

We also used to get lots of crabs in this area, 'Pillar' crabs at least that is what we called them , carrying baby crabs underneath them.

We got to know the tides and looked forward to Spring Tides especially on a windy day as the tide came in very high on these occasions and the waves really lashed the bottom of the

Cliff (there are some smaller cliffs but the high one was just referred to as The Cliff).

Further along the beach about a hundred yards or so going towards the First Lights (East Lights) was what was known as the Big Rock.

This Rock could probably tell a story or two. In the Summer this was a hub of activity as people from the other side of Tayport about a mile and a half away used to come here to paddle in the water or even to swim ( when the tide went out a beautiful sandy beach emerged at this point). This was most popular, not only with the locals but people from 'far off' Dundee.

The Dundonians would come over to spend the day in Tayport; they would get the Fifie - the Ferry from Dundee to Newport. I can remember 4 x names of the different Fifies

The B.L Nairn

Abercraig

Scotscraig

Sir William High

When the Dundonians got off the Fifie, they got a bus. I think it was a Bluebird, bus number 355, to Tayport and got off at Albert St., and came down Fairy Lane to the braes. You could hear them coming!

The Dundonians were very friendly and

good fun but very noisy! They came with
buckets and spades and great big bags with
no end of  interesting food for their picnic or
'shivery bite' (this was the treat after coming
out the water shivering, and with teeth
chattering).  They had  things like  Ingin or
( Onion ) Bridies - Irn Bru -Macaroon Bars -
Tablet - McCowans  Highland  Toffee Bars
( remember  this toffee with white  paper
wrapping and  a big highland cow on the
front! ) We had to make do with lemonade
bottles full of tap water and jam pieces that is
to say jam sandwiches.
The jam situation was that when you took a
bite of your piece, with the first bite you were
near the jam but with the next bite you had
passed it! Sometimes our sandwiches had
become foosty or (stale).

Dundee as the crow flies was only a few
miles away, but by Bus and Fifie it was about
5 or 6 miles.  (The Fifie had to make a longer
journey at low tide). When sailing from
Dundee it  had to sail down the river quite a
bit and then  curve in, steering towards
Newport from Dundee to avoid all the sand
banks and some sunken boats, the masts of
which  boats were  visible at low tide). If you
came by train it was about 9 x miles as the
train went to Wormit through Newport to

Tayport. Either way it wasn't too far but it could have been a hundred miles away to us, in fact overseas or over the river as far as visiting Dundee was concerned. We went about once a year or so if we were lucky.

All along the grassy part from the bottom of the Cliff, people used to lay out their blankets and makeshift windbreakers, like old umbrellas, ( usually black) to reserve their plot for the day .The men in their semmits ( vests ) with trousers rolled up to their knees.

We, the locals, used to look for whelks under the seaweed attached to the rocks. We had them for dinner. They were boiled in salt and we ate them with a safety pin.
This area by the Big Rock was also a good area to fish from; the men used to come down to the sandy beach and dig for bait. Then they would sling their hooks with lead sinkers on them and five or six hooks attached on their home made fishing lines.

The paddlers and swimmers had to manoeuvre between the fishing lines and try not to stand on the flooks or jelly fish swimming in the water!
Along still further, we came to a long rock

jutting out quite a few yards into the river. This rock was referred to as the Current Rock as there was a very strong current at the end of the rock. We were very careful to avoid this rock as it had been drummed in to us about the dangers.

I think the real name of the rock was the River Tay Rock.

River Tay Rock was only yards away from the First Lights (The First Lights is a listed building therefore the only work that is permitted is work to make it safe - no alterations as such). Apparently it was never painted and that is why it is not painted today due to the listed building restrictions.

Just after the First Lights there was another large rock; this was known as Cod Rock. Presumably because they caught cod there!

If we came up from the rocks at this point and joined the narrow road, we would find a fresh water spring on our right, about hundred yards before the Second Lights. Our very own pure water source! At least I hope so as we cupped our hands and drank from it often enough!

At the Second Lights there was a road on the left called Quarry Road. If you went up there you passed where there once was an overhead

**(SLEDGING)**

railway bridge. The trains went over there on the way to Dundee. The road was very narrow and winding). As you went up on the right you passed the quarry where many unusual birds were found. We even saw a peacock in full feather displayed there.

If you looked up to the main road from this area you would see a small hill. This was known as Cowslip Hill as it used to be covered with cowslips.

To the right of this hill about another 50 x yards stood Mercury Cottage. Continuing up Quarry Rd (see map at beginning of chapter) you came out almost on Albert St. and on your left was Braids Park or Braidsie.

This long and winding path was famous for one thing and one thing only - sledging. Crowds of bairns queued up to sledge down this hill which was usually a sheet of ice from top to bottom. At the bottom of the hill, when you were going at great speed, you had to turn left steering with your feet down about a dozen steps bumping all the way down. The sledge would come to a halt under another railway bridge.

The corner was very sharp and those not used to this area frequently went straight ahead at the top of the stairs over a very high ledge into a marshy area instead of turning left, as they couldn't control their sledges at such high speed.

If you didn't have a sledge then tin trays were used, but they were nowhere near as fast. There was and still is another area to the right of Braid's Park - a field or grassy area; running alongside the wall of this area was another sledge run. This was called the Camel's Hump and where the big boys sledged, as when you got to the bottom of this area, it came to an abrupt end. The field was on a raised level with quite a drop at the end of it. It was this drop that made it exciting as the sledge continued flying in the air for quite a way before you landed on the ground again, landing near some bushes or whins. Quite a few sledges were 'write offs' after landing here as they came down with such a force.

One young man, Peter Harley, had a sledge named the Iron Horse that was coveted by all the boys. (and some of us girls) It was very sturdy. I think it was made from a very old pram. This sledge without 'exaggeration' went faster than the speed of light - at least that was our opinion at the time!

On the left of Braid's Park was a large area absolutely covered in wild raspberry bushes free for all (this was at a different time of the year of course). There were always several people out here picking berries for jam. We used to take a big jam jar, fill it and take it home. This made the tastiest jam imaginable. There were also a few yellow rasps. We called those honey rasps. They were very sweet and their location kept secret by us of course!

Going down Braid's Park path again, down under the bridge you came to the Sandy Hole where people came with their families. They pitched their blankets and used this as their base when the bairns played in the Sandy Hole or went for a swim or (dook) in between. My friend and I had our favourite plot here. It was to the top right hand side where there were beautiful golden sands. We had to be there early to secure our favourite place.

If you moved up the road again towards the top of the cliff area, halfway up there was another very small quarry - like area. This was where my brother Stewart decided that if he 'made' a parachute, he could jump off here. This he did when my mother was at work in the mill. He 'borrowed' a bedspread off the bed and with a few adjustments jumped off this quarry area! Instead of slowing down the landing, it hastened the landing as the weight of the bedspread made him fall even more quickly!

If you continued back towards Fairy Lane you came back to Wellcraig house again where there was a narrow footpath that took you back to the Old Harbour. But if for the moment we don't take this route but continued on just past this house, we pass what was the Lemonade Works in Dalgliesh St., another play area for us! We used to collect the lovely different coloured bottle tops and take out he cork backing and fasten these 'badges ' to our blouses or tops. During this time many Polish people worked at the Lemonade Works. The neighbours spoke about talking to 'Poles'. This was very confusing for a young mind. The only Poles I knew were clothes poles or telegraph poles! The Lemonade Works  or aerated water company was originally owned by Melville's but in the later years was owned by Kidd and Co.  But to the locals it was always just known as Melville's.

At the braes end of the Lemonade Works there was an area that we the bairns used to look down on to the railway track. The track at this area was quite a drop from our vantage point as the track area had been hewn out of rock. One member of the group I was with namely, George Robertson fell down from this height on to the railway line, and 'split his head open' rendering him virtually unconscious.

Happily our screams were heard by Mr Maxwell from the Old Harbour who came rushing along and rescued George by giving him a 'cuddy back' to safety. The railway signal was down so a train was due any time on to this single railway track.

Just past the lemonade works was a foot bridge. Opposite this footbridge was a small hill or very large mound. There was an entrance at the bottom of this mound   I always believed this to be the entrance to an air raid shelter within this mound; the entrance was virtually opposite the footbridge. I remember being taken there. I must have only been three or four years old. There is now a house on this site. Unfortunately I have been unable to find anyone else who remembers this mound, my sister Irene remembers that there was something there. If we took the footbridge across the railway, this brought us out to the Old Harbour.

## Old Harbour

The Old Harbour was also a favourite area for swimmers as it seemed safer than the New Harbour. This perception was false as both were extremely dangerous. There was a long pier with a square end. To the right of this pier was a sandy harbour area. This was the most used part of the harbour. Some of us jumped off the edge of the pier but couldn't really swim as the water was quite deep and way out of our depth; all we knew was the doggie's paddle. We surfaced after jumping in and then did the doggie's paddle in between the boat ropes.

Mr Maxwell who lived at the Old Harbour had two boats moored there, one being the Tay Queen in which he used to go up the river to catch seals.
He was employed by Tay Fisheries to cull seals the other boat was called the Daisy (the Daisy was called after his daughter) At low tide the seals used to play on the sand banks near the Tay Rail Bridge.

In the corner of this part of the harbour was what we considered to be our own Marie Celeste- the Princess Arthur .This boat was

the subject of much conjecture. It was quite a
wreck and seemed to arrive from nowhere. It
was moored in the harbour for several years
with nothing seeming to be done with it.
Apparently it was owned by the owner of a
Company called Brand and Rae from
Springfield near Cupar.

The water in this area was considered to be
therapeutic. A neighbour from Isla place
used to come down to the harbour and dip her
infant son in the harbour, whatever the
weather, to heal his eczema. The water was
icy cold and he screamed his head off most of
the time.
There was a short cut from the Old Harbour
to Dalgliesh St., by the footbridge as
previously mentioned, and there was also
another short cut a little further along
through the wickety gates over the railway
lines at Inn St., bringing you out near the Ice
House in Dalgliesh St.,

## The New Harbour
The New Harbour was a very busy area
during my childhood. Word went round like
wildfire when a Wood Boat delivering wood
came in. Some of these boats were about 300

feet long almost the whole length of the harbour! These boats came in regularly from places like Holland and Norway to deliver wood. When they were sailing up the Tay with their cargo on board, the ships looked as if they were going to sink. They were so far down in the water with most of them on and almost below their Plimsoll line.

(The Plimsoll line is a loading mark painted on to the hull of Merchant Ships, first suggested by the 19th Century politician Samuel Plimsoll. It shows the depth to which a vessel may be safely and legally loaded). We, the bairns, were very interested in the people, but not the wood. We were fascinated with these foreigners. At school we were used to names like Jimmy, Peem, Alec etc., but their names sounded much more interesting like -Jorgen -
Helmut - Wolfgang- and Hans (I cannot recall anyone called feets though)!

**Air Sea Rescue**
The Air Sea Rescue was based in Tayport from about 1943 until 1958. The Tayport division of the Air Sea Rescue came under the supervision of RAF Leuchars about 6 x miles away.
There were two beautiful 43 ft long speed boats or launches moored in the harbour from

about 1953 until 1958. Prior to this there was
at least one launch a smaller one namely a 41
ft long launch. This slightly smaller type of
boat was used throughout the war years from
1943 onwards. These boats formed part of the
Air Sea Rescue which was based in Billets
just behind the Coal Drop. The speed boats
went extremely fast leaving a trail of white
horses in the water behind them.

According to Mr. Terry Lloyd who was a
coxswain on one these type of launches, the
43 ft long boats could cruise at 27 knots, this
is about 30 miles per hour (one knot is just
over 1 x miles per hour). The speed would
always be governed by sea conditions.

Calm seas equal high speed, rough seas equal
slower speeds.

Similar boats were stationed in harbours in
strategic areas around the British Isles. The
purpose of these boats and others like them
was to rescue Air Crews from the sea when
they were being forced down into the sea. In
fact the Air Sea Rescue was like a massive
R.N.L.I. Service and was on call for any
emergency all around the British Isles.

The airmen who manned these speed boats
were ready at a moment's notice to speed out
to sea in some life or death drama.

Interestingly these bands of specialised men
were actually *sailors* in the R.A.F, specially

trained for Air Sea Rescue. These people were responsible for rescuing over 15,000 Air Crew personnel from the North Sea and English Channel. The camaraderie amongst these sailors was such that a club was formed in 1950 for A.S.R. crews which still have over 1,000 members today.

There was a very large Hangar at the top of the Slip for the boats to be serviced or repaired. This was situated to the left of the Coal Drop facing the mouth of the harbour. The Slip is still there but the Hangar has long gone. We and many people before us swam in this Slip area. It was very popular with the swimmers but annoying no doubt for those with yachts and small boats. The swimmers swam between the mooring ropes.

I have included some pictures in the photo gallery at the back of this book.

1. A speed boat in the harbour showing the Billets in the background
2. The large Boat Hangar
3. Inside the Boat Hangar
4. Inside the Billets.

Incidentally prior to the RAF using the Billets they were apparently occupied by German Prisoners of War.

## MUSSEL BOATS

Mussel boats were usually moored at the railway station side of the harbour; there were still a few boats operating at this time.

## DREDGER

A large Dredger used to come in the harbour to dredge the mud and silt. This kept the harbour safe for the large boats coming in so that they would not get stuck in the mud. The Dredgers were extremely ugly boats; Nonetheless we were very pleased to see them arrive.

## THE SCHOTTER

The Schotter was a yacht that came in to the harbour regularly I believe the owners were from Wormit. It was a very familiar sight. Everyone knew the Schotter. The owners were very pleasant.

## COAL DROP

The Coal Drop was a tall building in the harbour where steamships would come for re-fuelling. The coal drop was no longer in use at the time I remember but I have lasting memories of bairns using this as a diving board . They dived from the loading platform, they were actually diving into a very busy harbour area, and it was extremely dangerous.

One young local boy, Ian Rennie, when he was about 14 x years old dived from the <u>roof</u> of this coal drop, that was another 20ft or so higher than the platform. This was very frightening to watch. He stood on the corner of the roof for a little while before actually diving off. The dive was spectacular. He was like a bird. It was a highly dangerous thing to do but no one could stop him.

The height of this dive was about 45 ft from the top of the Coal Drop to the water. The tide was actually quite low so he dived in to very shallow water.

## PODLES

Not sure about the spelling of this word but many of us went fishing for 'podles'. They were very small fish, not much bigger than minnows .We used to catch them for the cat (although none of us had a cat)!

We fished for these down the steps just outside the Harbour Master's office, near where the Wood Boats moored.

Have you noticed that fish looking suspiciously like   these podles are served as a delicacy on some A.L.C Menu's in Restaurants under the name of WHITEBAIT?

If we continued down from the New Harbour past the Harbour Master's office, we passed along by the wood yard the storage area for all the planks of wood that had been unloaded from the wood boats. This wood belonged to the owners of the Sawmill.

For us of course it was another place to play but fraught with danger. The Gaffer nicknamed Whiskery Dick would come along and threaten us if we didn't move as we were jumping from stack to stack. Some of these stacks must have been about 15 ft high the planks of wood were loose so when we jumped on the pile of planks the planks used to move precariously, if they had come down on us we would have been crushed and not lived to tell the tale.

After this area we came to the Common. The swings and the ocean wave in the play area were very popular but a bit tame for us tomboys. There was of course a boating pond with paddle boats where you sat in the boat and propelled it with handles either side. There were also the rowing boats. We developed quite a speed rowing these; it was 3d for 15 x minutes. There was an old man who sat in what was like a sentry box in the top left hand corner facing the pond. He was in charge. He blew and blew and blew again on his whistle to get us to row back in and hand over the boats to someone else in the queue. The whistle blew on deaf ears. We used to deliberately lose an oar so that it wouldn't be our fault if we were late in with the boat , thereby giving us longer than our allocated 15 x minutes.

Continuing on past the Common, you past the coup (or rubbish dump), then past the Canniepart Burn on down to fascinating Tentsmuir, namely the Moors on the edge of the Estuary.

*See picture gallery at back of book for a picture of the Estuary

The Moors have a long history well documented in other books. Rich in wild life with miles of Golden Sands and a Commercial Forest

The Tayport people have always treasured this area.

A popular stop there was the first large Sand Dune it was like another large sandy hole. Here again was another picnic area.

Our parents and grandparents also used to come here for picnics and to swim in the river. I have a picture of my mother at this same Sand Dune when she was about 20 years old. This would have been in about the year 1923.

An interesting point about this area is that according to my father, the tide comes in from <u>seven</u> different directions. This is because of the currents and streams. Anyone who has been out to Lucky Scaup,  the island in the Estuary, knows what happens here…

The tide goes out for what seems to be miles. It is certainly a great distance. If for example if you stood on the shore and looked out to Lucky Scaup, you would find it difficult to see someone wave to you if they were there. When the tide comes in it virtually chases you in. You almost have to run to get back safely and as the tide comes in from all these directions, it is coming in from your side as well as behind you.

The reverse is true too. If you are paddling or swimming, the tide runs out almost like someone pulling a plug out and you have to chase it to keep up with it!

This was, and is, one of the few places in the Country, where this phenomenon occurred. One of the good points of this was that the water was very shallow at this point and so was quite warm here because the sandy beach underneath was very hot from the sun and this kept it fairly warm. It was like swimming in the bath.

All along the coast there were Cement Pillars or Anti - Tank Defences. These were to prevent tanks from landing during the war. These pillars were square with a slightly rounded top they must have been about 5ft high.

The pillars  two rows of them which were slightly offset to each other to make  it extremely difficult for tanks to land there, started from just about the area of the wood yard down to the sea wall, then continuing a little way along from the sea wall all the way to virtually the First Point. (The First Point was the furthest point of Tentsmuir like a peninsula jutting out in the Estuary almost level with the Bar of the Tay).  The total of these Cement Pillars or Anti Tank Defences must have amounted to hundreds.

* See picture gallery for picture of some of these Cement Pillars.

Incidentally if you continued to end of the First Point and turned the corner you would soon reach Eden.

 (Not the Garden of Eden but the River Eden)!

Coming back up from the Moors, we came across the Mill ( Tayport Spinning Mill ). This provided employment for hundreds of

local people It was a Jute Mill (Dundee our near neighbour, was famous as they say for Jute, Jam and Journalism). This was just known as the Mill. People worked extremely hard here from 7.30 am until 5.30pm.
The people came out of the gates in their droves, ten abreast like a football crowd bursting out. Everyone was on foot and many had a very long walk indeed ahead of them to their respective homes. My mother referred to 'tramping cans' as one of the duties that she had to perform whilst working in the Mill.

Coming up Nelson St., you passed what was known as Factory Corner. The Factory mentioned here belonged to Scott & Fyfe. It too was a Jute factory this time a weaving factory. It provided employment for many of the local people.

Many of us will remember the day this factory virtually burned down to the ground with only a small part, namely the original part remaining. The fire started or was discovered about 5.30 pm in the evening minutes if not seconds after the last workers had left for home. The alarm was raised by some residents in Nelson St.,
Fire broke out in the calender shop of this factory the name of the factory was actually

Scott & Fyfes Jute Works. The extent of the fire was such that the estimated cost of the fire was £100,000 that was the headline in the next day's Dundee Courier. I cannot imagine what that would be in today's money!

My sister Irene was working there that day and she had not come home from work. There was an incredible amount of smoke billowing out all over the town from the fire. The call went out and spread like wild fire that the factory was on fire. With Irene being late we feared that she was in there, but she had gone up to the shops immediately after work to buy some socks for my brother Stewart for his birthday that day.
Namely Friday 11th May 1956.
The Factory amazingly was soon up and running again. Later like many others in the Jute industry it diversified and began using polypropylene

If you looked to the right from Factory corner you would have seen yet another railway bridge that we walked under to get to the Common this bridge was known as the Plouter.
If you came up to Queen St you came across the Picture House situated at the bottom of King St.

The picture house is mentioned in a bit more detail in a further chapter of this book.

Castle St., the main shopping area or 'up the town' was just off the corner of Queen St. THERE WERE APPROXIMATELY X 40 SHOPS in Tayport at this time!

## TAYPORT SHOPS

Starting from Broad St., in to Castle St.,
SCOTT'S -the Newsagent and Sweetie Shop -
GRAHAME'S - the Butcher
SIMPSONS -Newsagents Sweetie& toy shop
CLYDESDALE BANK
PEEBLES –Grocers
WILKIE'S- Drapers
GILCHRISTS -Bakers
SMITH AND KAY -Shoe Shop and Cobblers
WOOL SHOP
McGREGOR'S - The Chemist
MATT GORDON -Jewellers
LESLIE -Barbers
Wm LOW -Grocery shop
NANCY GREIG- Sweetie Shop
ADAMS - Sweetie Shop
WULLIE FAIRLIE -Barbers
GRAHAME AND GIBB-Bakers
HAIRDRESSER
CLARKES - Book shop ?
MaCRAES -Sold gloves etc.,- Little Café
POST OFFICE

RATTRAY'S - Grocer
AUCHTERLONIE'S -Fruit & Veg
LEONARD SMITH'S - Ironmongers
GUNN - Fishmongers
GUNN - Butcher
 McFARLANE  - Bakers
YOUNGS - Grocers
PILLANS/CUTHBERT- Plumbers
DUNDEE SAVINGS BANK
WILKIE'S- Home Furnishings
CABRELLI'S- Fish & Chip Shop
*** 

WULLIE DUTHIE'S - Queen St
 COSS (Cosies) Elizabeth St
AULDIE'S- Shanwell Rd
STORE / CO-OP- Nelson St
GRIEG'S Bakers Cross St
ARTHUR BLACK'S Henderson's St ?
JOE BARBIERI Fish & Chip Shop-Nelson St.,
ANGUS BARBIERI -Young People's Cafe
MISS BARCLAY- Maitland St ?
ROBERTSON'S-Greenside Place
ELLA McGREGOR - Ogilvy St.,
VAVRO - Bookshop Pond Lane
BARBEIRI'S - Nelson St.,
WYLES - Pond Lane
HADDON WAINMAN -William St.,
BUTCHERS- Tay St

Continuing along Queen St and turning left
up William St., until you got to Spears Hill,
from the top of here just along the footpath to

your left was the point that you got the best view of the Estuary. (We could also get to this point from Victoria Rd going up past Jack Clarke's dairy on the left). The fascinating thing here, due to the width and clear unobstructed view of the Estuary, was that you could experience what ancient mariners and historians experienced when they saw a ship approaching from a distance-first of all the mast of a ship coming up, then the rest of the ship coming up what would appear to be a hill. This helped us to actually see that the world was round. This was of course a corroborating fact as the shape of the earth's shadow on the moon during an eclipse was considered by Aristotle to be evidence that the world was round. The sun rising up from the 'water' was another phenomenon, seen very clearly from here as we looked out on to the horizon at the estuary.

Tayport has an unusual claim to fame because it has arguably one of the most beautiful last resting places in the country. The Cemetery here is on a slight slope going down, with the River Tay, the Second Lights, and Broughty Ferry Castle in the background with the river Tay meandering towards the mouth of the river.

## 'BRITANNIA RULED THE WAVES' - TO DUNDEE

On Friday October the 7$^{th}$ 1955 Dundee
harbour officials were informed that the
Royal Yacht Britannia would berth   in
Dundee and stay there until the Monday
October the 10$^{th}$.
During her voyage from Portsmouth
Britannia was caught up in strong gales so
had to reduce her speed. A message was sent
out to say that she would arrive 3 x hours
late.
'Britannia ruled the waves' and managed to
arrive on time to her original schedule.
The Britannia berthed in the Queen Elizabeth
Wharf. Later in the evening she looked
spectacular as she was brilliantly floodlit.
The boat moored in silence as in accordance
with Royal Yacht Britannia tradition any
orders must be issued in signs!   The scores
of seamen had to wear sandshoes or
plimsolls. Captain John Walker the
harbourmaster, supervised the berthing.


The Queen and Duke were spending the
weekend at Meikleour then boarding
Britannia on the Monday to take them to
Copenhagen for the British Trade Fair.

My mother and I watched this on the Monday and admired the beautiful sight of seeing the Britannia sail or glide down the Tay.

The Britannia was 412 feet 3 inches long.

## FESTIVAL OF BRITAIN

On Wednesday the 16th May 1951 the Campania a 540 feet long converted aircraft carrier berthed at Dundee. This was quite something the boat was referred to as "A SHINING COLOSSUS OF THE SEA"

This was in a year not too long after the end of the Second World War when rationing was still required so this Festival spirit was welcomed. We were made aware of this at school so the arrival of the Campania was heralded by the Tayport people as we stared at the horizon seeing just a mast then gradually the whole ship come in to sight...

The Captain was also in the Festival mood as when the boat passed us it gave a very long siren blast. What excitement!

See picture at the back of this book of the Campania actually berthing in Queen Elizabeth Wharf with several other ships in the Dundee docks in the background.

I hope you will enjoy the following chapters of this book seeing life through the eyes of a Tayport bairn just after the 2nd World War.

# CHAPTER THREE
## (Berry Picking)

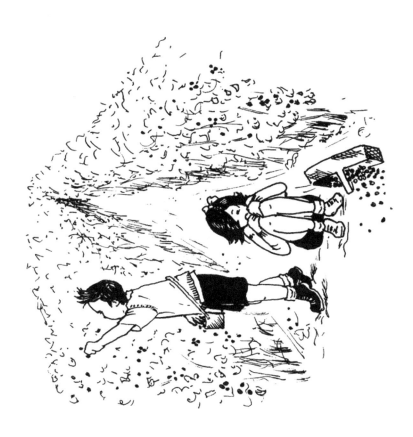

# A DAY AT THE BERRIES

In our school holidays it was very popular for the children to go to the berries (picking rasps) to make some money. A big open lorry used to come and pick us up and go to Pittormie, a farm just outside Dairsie about 6 miles from Tayport. While travelling we used to sing songs like " I'm going on the train and your no comin wi' me; ah've got a lad o ma ain and his name is kiltie Jeemie" or "How much is that doggie in the window" to the latter it was accompanied all the way with the boys woofing and barking like animals in distress.

There were long 'dreels' with the berry bushes absolutely towering above our heads. We had to pick the rasps and put them in a little bucket or pail tied around our waists called a ' luggie ', presumably so named because we had to lug this bucket about. We filled the luggie by which time we were bent almost double as the luggie was weighing heavily round our waists. We then had to empty the contents of the luggie in to our big bucket. We were not too happy if the bucket was too far away from us as others might pinch it, including all the berries that we had spent hours and hours on picking.

At the end of each day you had to try to lift this heavy bucket and carry it to the weighing machine in a corner of the berry field. These buckets needed Desperate Dan to lift them. It was almost impossible for us bairns to do so. However we managed to get them to the weighing machine by carrying the buckets a few feet at a time, then having a wee rest, then rubbing our backs and carrying on a further few yards. There was a long queue of people bent almost double trying to carry these big buckets towards the weighing machine. When carrying them the weight of them almost made you go in to a three step trot and drop the bucket. We were very keen to find out how much we had made, that is to say our earnings for the day. What happened frequently was that when we eventually got to the weighing machine much to our dismay our buckets tipped over spilling the berries on the ground! We would make sure that the Gaffer did not see us then pick them up with a fell swoop, scooping them up in our hands hoping that nobody else saw us either and continue towards the pay weighing machine. The berries were all squashed and mushy - yuk! Some scallywags resorted to putting some wee boulders in among the berries so that they would weigh a bit more.

The most that I made in a day was 4 -

shillings and 10d pence, old pence.

I was asked by a kindly woman how much I had earned and when I said 4 and 10 she said "What do you mean you dinnae ken? You have just been paid (she was actually English and mistook 4 and 10 for dinnae ken-) she thought I was being insolent!!

There was a lot of fun at the berries but it was extremely hard work.

The first picking of the berries in the dreels was the best, as the bushes were laden with berries and you could pick the berries and fill your luggie   fairly quickly so we made a little more money on these days.

Some days (we hated those days) you had to go back to the fields and dreels that you had already worked on first picking, and go second or even third picking to pick the few berries that had grown in the last few days or we had missed on the last picking.

This was hard work. The Gaffer would come along and push the bushes back with his  big stick and let out a loud roar  and in no uncertain terms call us back to pick the few berries that we had missed  usually at the top of the bushes or along the bottom. The price we were paid per pound varied. You got a little more per pound on second or third picking.

Even by getting more per pound on these days  we never earned nearly as much as we would have done on the first picking. News that we were second picking the following day went round like wild fire with everyone moaning and groaning and threatening not to come in the next day (they always did of course).

We were quite nauseous or should I say felt 'seek' by the end of each day as we had usually eaten all  our ' pieces' very early, probably by 10 am. The knowledge of our jam pieces just sitting in our piece bag that we brought for lunch burnt a hole in our 'stomach', so we ate them at that time. Sometimes we ate them on the lorry before we arrived!  - So we had to eat the berries to fill us up!! Some *even* ate their lunch at the lorry stop whilst waiting for the lorry to arrive to take them to work early in the morning! Next day of course like lemmings we were up with the lark to take us back with renewed vigour to catch the lorry to take us back yet another day.

WE WERE A LITTLE " PAIL" BY THE END OF THE DAY

By the way I hope you enjoyed your Jam best vintage 1952

# CHAPTER FOUR
## ( COAL FIRES AND CLOOTIE DUMPLINGS)

# COAL FIRES AND CLOOTIE DUMPLINGS

At the end of each day it was great to be home.

Nearly everyone had a coal fire - we had an open range. This was my mother's pride and joy. The oven was polished with black lead. The particular polish that was used was zebo. Mother polished this nearly every day until it shone like a mirror - mind you half the polish was on her face and nose, and the rest was on the grate!

The coal fire was quite deep with a grid in front of it so you could see the layers of cinders when the fire was at its height. The cinders were all glowing as well. The flames used to really crackle, gigantic flames going up the lum. The fire was a most welcome sight. We sat round this fire getting hotter and hotter that is to say our fronts got hotter and hotter but our backs got colder and colder. It was reckoned that if we opened the windows we would let the heat in from the outside to warm our backs!

Some of the older women in the town had what we called tartan legs as their legs were semi- permanently burnt from the fire. It was a red mottled look that never seemed to go away. Do you remember this?

This may have happened to the men as well but their trousers would have protected their legs - unless they wore kilts of course!

We also toasted our bread at the fire with a fork. We had to keep changing hands as we would be yelping with the pain from the heat travelling up the fork! The toast got smaller and smaller as the bread used to break where we had inserted the fork. The toast would fall to the ground so we had to make another hole with the remaining piece of bread - another hole and another hole.....and yet *another* hole. Sometimes you were left just toasting the crust! (Plain George or curly Kate). Incidentally it was usually only toasted on one side. You couldn't do that process again with the other side as there would be no bread left at all!

My sister Irene, an avid reader, considered herself an expert at making black treacle toffee. She used to make this whilst reading a book. Consequently every kitchen utensil with a flat bottom was covered in a thick black lining where the toffee was burned. Pots, pans and ashets were all covered in this black toffee; even a hammer and chisel could not remove it!

My favourite food was the clootie dumpling. It was on the stove for hours and hours - and was usually wrapped in a dish towel. When it was ready with a lovely thick skin, we used to watch and wait while the cloth was peeled off the dumpling. The end result was a very dark clootie dumpling big much bigger than a large loaf of bread. We had it cold. WE EVEN HAD IT FRIED if there was any left!

I have listed some of the most common food or meals we had at the time - some of course still eaten today -.
Potted Hough -Tripe and Onions- Stovies  -
Saps    ( bread and milk ) Tatties and Mince with dough 'boys' (balls)
and another more unusual, called Rumeldithump. This was made basically from fried oatmeal and onions. For pudding what about Creamola?
Of course on many days for some of us it was just bread margarine and sugar.

# CHAPTER FIVE
## (THE BELT)

# THE BELT

Who of us can forget The Belt!
Not many of us managed to escape the
dreaded belt .The belt was the ultimate
deterrent. It was about 3and a half feet long 2
and a half inches wide with three tails at the
end and made from leather.
When it was not in use it was curled up like a
cobra waiting to pounce on its prey.
When you got the belt it was usually more
than one lash probably from one to six lashes.
I got the belt frequently. Some teachers
'only' gave you the belt on one hand -we had
to hold out our hand away from us at our
side. This was bad enough but some teachers
insisted that you put two hands together i.e.
one hand on top of the other.
The fingers of the bottom hand would
protrude from under the top hand so when
you got the belt it stung both hands reaching
all your fingers. The pain was excruciating.
We let out a loud wail then went back to our
seats with our hands under our oxters
(armpits) to try to relieve the pain.
If we had tried to pull our hands away in fear,
then that meant that we would get an extra
lash for each time we pulled our hand away.
The teacher would bring the strap down with

great gusto from his or her shoulder while one foot was raised then   landing on it when the blow was given in a stance that would rival Olympic Javelin throwers.  This was brought down on to our trembling hands!!! I got the belt for 'sniggering' or for my bad handwriting. The handwriting became worse because of this as my hands shook in fear when writing.  To quote this teacher my handwriting was like 'hens' foot prints all over the page - incidentally it is still like hens' foot prints all over the page.

 This teacher was nicknamed Hippo.

The teachers rarely succeeded in hitting just our hands. The tails of the belt usually hit you on the soft part of your wrist causing three tailed swelling almost drawing blood.

One teacher, my sewing teacher, appeared to have an intense dislike of me. One day I accidentally knocked over a box of tacking pins with my yardstick and all the pins scattered over the floor - well Miss F 'lost her rag' - and gave me the belt with such force that she completely missed my hand and the belt hit me from the wrist to the elbow, the horrific weal from this lasted for about a week. It was swollen and dark red (I was about 12 at the time).

How I managed to hide this from my mother

I will never know. What I do know is that if she had seen this, Miss F, the sewing teacher, would have had to become familiar with another type of stitch HOSPITAL STITCH.

# CHAPTER SIX
## (DOUBLERS)

# Familiar Sounds, Sayings & Ditties

## Eechie nor Ochie
Example- if someone was recalling a situation and wanted the hearer to know that they had made no comment at the time to which they were referring, would say "I didnae say neither eechie nor ochie".

## Lucky Scaup to Bide a Tide
Referring to the fact that they could not afford a holiday they said ( referring to the tiny Lucky Scaup Island in the Tay Estuary) - " I'm awa tae Lucky Scaup to Bide a Tide" (only of course a very short stay, about 12 hours 25 minutes, the duration of a tide).

## The Call of Wullie Doctor the Fruit and Veg Man
Fruit and Vegetables were sold from door to door. This was usually delivered by horse and cart.

The Tayport people had their very own unique delivery man namely Wullie Doctor. He looked a bit like Paw Broon from the Broons in the Sunday Post, he used to arrive outside Isla 'Place with his horse and cart and let out a mighty roar!! DOAC -TURR! Nothing else. Just DOAC-TURR!

My Auntie Jean from Glasgow was visiting

one day and was alarmed by this very loud call of DOAC -TURR! She was convinced that someone was calling for help!

## Men Whistling Complete Tunes Walking Down the Street

Men whistled long and complicated tunes. Lots of Scottish tunes preferred e.g. The Bluebell Polka -The Hundred Pipers a' an a'- Katie Bairdie had a Coo. Wi' a Toorie on his Bonnet,
Stop your tickling Jock - The Northern Lights of old Aberdeen - I belong to Glesca (Glasgow).
Lots of men had their 'theme' tune. My father always whistled 'Cuckoo Cuckoo cu coo cu coo cu coo cu cu ca coo' repeatedly.

## Mill Peep or Whistle

The Mill Workers were summoned to work by means of a loud long peep, a bit like a siren. In the morning it went off at approx 7.10 am ( the first peep ) then at approx 7.25am ( the second or last peep) then at 12 noon to break up for lunch, then 12.40 pm and 12.55 pm to come back to work. Most of the workers had a long way to walk to work as there were virtually no cars.

## We are 'a ' Jock Tamson's Bairns

This was a great leveller. If anyone got carried away with their own importance they were reminded that we all come from a common source, that is to say , we are a' Jock Tamson's bairns.

## Haud your wheesht (whisht )

'Say no more' usually in a light hearted manner - e. g.  Och haud your wheesht. Other times it was said as a rebuke to get people to be quiet.

## Whit a fleg

What a fright! This expression is still commonly used today. It is more colourfully descriptive than what a fright!

## Sleekit

Underhanded and devious, frequently referring to someone who appears to be nice but who is slyly thinking and planning something else.

## Glaikit

Word meaning that you are more than stupid. No other word describes empty headedness or being gormless as well as this word.

## Peely Wally
If someone was a bit off colour and looking a bit white, it was said "you are looking awfy peely wally"

## But and Ben
A two roomed cottage; But - the outer room. Ben -the inner room.

## Mony a  Mickle maks a Muckle -
Many small amounts accumulate to make a large amount.

## Canny Hear Ahent a Ha'penny Biscuit
Referring to the fact that they could hardly hear something, perhaps the radio or someone with a soft voice. (ahent a ha'penny biscuit = behind a  thin  halfpenny biscuit)

## If you Canny Dae Somebody a GoodTurn, Dinnae Dae Them a Bad Turn.
Local version of the golden rule.

# SONGS AND DITTIES

I'm a wee melody man ( meloady)
A rufty tufty toady man
I always do the best I can to follow
my wee melody man.
***

My wee Jeannie
Has a nice clean peenie
And guess what colour it was
(e.g pink) P-I-N-K spells pink and pink you
must have on.
***

On the mountain stands a lady
Who she is I do not know
All she wants is gold and silver
All she wants is a nice young man
So call in my sister……..
Sister…..
As I go out to play
***

A house to let
Apply within
As I go out
My neighbour comes in
***

Black sugar white sugar
Strawberry Jam
Tell me the name of your young man
A B C D E F G etc.
***

Mrs Delop she had a wee shop
And all she sold was candy rock
Candy rock a penny a stalk
All she sold was candy rock.
***

# CHAPTER SEVEN
## (KICK THE CAN)

# ENTERTAINMENT

## The McFlannels

Who can remember the McFlannels?
Saturday night entertainment on the home
service- we used to run home to hear this
play.
The McFlannels was an amusing account of
life in Glasgow. The characters were made up
from people with surnames of different
fabrics. For example, McFlannel, McTweed ,
McCotton  and added later McCrepe.
The programme was based on a working-
class Glasgow family and their friends and
neighbours. They all had surnames with this
material or fabric connection.
There was a frightfully posh and pan-loafie
woman who lived next door to the
McFlannels. She featured quite a bit in the
weekly stories.

There was Maisie - Sadie - Wullie and
Grandad. Grandad was known for saying - ae
me my mi mo a never deed a winter yet!

## RADIO PROGRAMMES

### It's All Yours

 Stanley Baxter and Jimmy Logan -. Jimmy
had a character called Sammy Dreep.

## Dick Barton Special Agent
Exploits of Dick, Jock and Snowy.

## Radio Luxembourg
Pete Murray 208 on the Medium Wave

## Take it from here
Jimmy Edwards - Dick Bentley - Joyce Nichols (the Glum family).  June Whitfield joined the cast later and became Dick's Fiancée -'Eth and Ron'

## Family favourites
Cliff Michelmore and Jean Metcalfe. The theme tune was – "A song in my heart".

## Billy Cotton Band show -wakey wakeeeee
Sunday lunchtime series from 1949 until 1968. His theme tune was "Somebody stole my Gal"

## Mrs Dale's Diary
Still worried about Jim!

## Top of the Form
Quiz -with school teams competing against each other.
## Have a go Joe, come and have a go
Wilfred Pickles and his wife Mabel "Ow much money on the Table Mabel".

## Life with the Lyons
Ben Lyon and Bebe Daniels -Domestic
Comedy.

## Educating Archie
Peter Brough ventriloquist and his dummy
Archie Andrews.

## Rays a Laugh
Ted Ray and Kitty Bluett
The King of the One Liners.

## Music while you work
This was first broadcast on the wireless in
June 1940 and was played to British Factory
workers with a view to increase wartime
productivity and morale. By the end of the
war there were over 5 x million people tuning
in! The programme ended when the Light
Programme came off the air in 1967

## Jimmy Jewell and Ben Warris
Similar style to Abbott and Costello

## Arthur Askey
Big Hearted Arthur (Hello Playmates)

## Lift Up Your Hearts
Scriptural thought for the day

## GAMES WE PLAYED
(STREET GAMES)
Leerevo
Kick the Can
Hoist the Flag
Tracking
Chappie Doorie (knocking at doors and running away)
Beddies or - Peevers (Hopscotch)
Walk the Plank or Join the Crew.
You Can't Cross the River
Doublers.

## Pop? Songs
Gilly Gilly Osenfeffer
Cherry Pink and Apple Blossom white
Rosemarie - By Slim Whitman
 I see   the Moon -the Moon sees me
Pickin a Chicken
I wonder who's kissing her now.
Happy Wanderer
How much is that Doggie in the Window
Bye Bye Blackbird
Dear Hearts and Gentle people
If you're in Arizona I'll follow you (if you're in- Minnesota I'll be there too my heart cries for you)
Oh Mein Papa
She wears my ring
Chickery Chick. Chilie Chilie

# CHAPTER EIGHT
## (STEAM TRAINS)

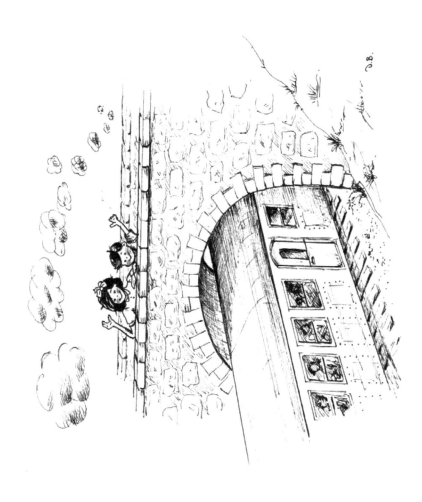

# STEAM TRAINS AND THE TAY BRIDGE

We had beautiful steam trains. They were a wonderful sight; however often we saw these trains, we were always very excited to see them. We would stop whatever we were doing and a loud shout would go up THE TRAIN'S COMING! THE TRAIN'S COMING! We would wave enthusiastically and the passengers would do the same; somehow everyone seemed friendlier then than they are today.

Some railway bridges over pathways were really quite low so we used to run to get under the bridge to hear the 'thunder', the noise trains made as they ran over the bridge. The trains from Tayport went to Dundee stopping at - East Newport- West Newport - Wormit- then Dundee Tay Bridge Station.

We lived very near the Railway station. When the trains left the station there was a certain rhythm to the sound of the engine pulling away. As it was pulling away after about 100 yards or so, the driver would sound the whistle; this was just level with our house.

Some of the engine drivers blew their whistle especially for us as they passed by.

We, as already mentioned lived close to the station so, on a rainy day, we played in the waiting room. We got friendly with the drivers and some of them let us on to the engine itself (before it took off). We got to shovel the coal on to the furnace.

The route described above was very scenic from the railway line. You could see the beautiful Tay all the way from Tayport to Dundee.

The river Tay with Wormit on one side and Dundee on the other side is about two miles wide.

Going across the rail bridge was quite something, with spectacular views on both sides of the bridge. Looking to the East you looked towards the Estuary taking in the sights of Tayport and Broughty Ferry . To the West you looked up river towards Perth taking in views of the Sidlaw Hills.

The first Rail Bridge was constructed and finished by February 1878. The bridge only lasted 19 months in total.  On a stormy night on 28th December 1879 the bridge collapsed while a passenger train was crossing. The train and all the passengers went in to the icy cold river and all the people were drowned, 75 in total.

There have been many theories as to why the bridge fell down. The one that is most widely accepted is that the engineer did not take into account the gales from the Tay Estuary .The night the bridge went down there was an estimated gale at force 10 to 11 coming up the Tay at right angles to the bridge.

The designer of the bridge, Thomas Bouch, at the time of the disaster was working on the design for the proposed Forth Bridge !!!

It was decided to transfer the bridge design of that project to Benjamin Baker and Sir John Fowler. Otherwise we may have had another disaster!

A new bridge was built along side where the old Tay Bridge was built - (you can still see the supports of the old bridge reaching out of the river).

We were always very nervous going over the bridge when we were on the train,   especially on a windy night!

The trip from Tayport to Dundee on the steam train, in spite of this fear, was sheer joy. The carriages had individual compartments with seating for approx x 6/8 passengers. The doors were opened by us pulling up a leather strap to let the window down so we could open the door by using the outside door handle.

Many of us will remember the tragedy of the Sunday school picnic train that crashed in the Wormit Tunnel on Saturday 28th May 1955. Two men and one young boy were killed; the total of those injured numbered x 42. They had been on a Sunday school picnic to Tayport Common. The train was absolutely crowded; it was a special picnic train for three Churches in Dundee St Ninians, St Andrews Parish and Morison Church in Dundee the total number of people on board was about 500. (250 children and 250 adults.) My friend and I remembered this, particularly as Mr Low, who was the engine driver, had been talking to us in the station waiting room area and he was one of the casualties.

There was a long white mark along the side of the tunnel indicating that the engine or carriage scraped along the wall of the tunnel before the train actually crashed. This mark was visible for a long time afterwards; we saw this every time we travelled on the train to Dundee.

(It is significant to mention here to those not familiar with Wormit Station and its location is the fact that this was situated just at the approach to the Tay Rail Bridge. The River Tay was on the right with almost a sheer drop from the station down to the water, from

quite a considerable height)
 Had the engine left the line 50 yards further
on it would have landed in the River Tay
taking all the passengers with them!

When the Tay Road Bridge was opened by
the   Queen Mother on the 18th August 1966
there was no further need for the train
service.

# CHAPTER NINE
## (TATTIE PICKING)

# HERE COMES THE TATTIE PICKERS!

As was customary when we were about 14 years old, we were allowed three weeks off school to go to the tattie (potato) picking. We really looked forward to doing this as it was a great opportunity to earn some money. We actually hated the work but enjoyed being off school and the thought of the money was very exciting.

We had no say in where we would go to the tattie picking. Various farms were signed up to take us.

I was assigned to a Farm just outside St Andrews called Kincaple. I see this Farm every time I drive in to St Andrews now. There were several fields planted with potatoes. One in particular was on what appeared to be a steep hill. This hill is parallel with the main road in to St Andrews.

Anyone who has picked potatoes will remember how back breaking it was. You were soon on your knees gathering the potatoes, pulling a heavy creel along through your legs.

This was in October and there was usually a frost or rime early in the morning. The frost was on the ground and we were frozen stiff before we started.

Sometimes it was hard to tell the difference between potatoes and white frosted stones.

We tried to make it fun by singing as we picked, but this didn't last long. The only sounds were "oh! ma back or what time is it? Is it no dinner time yet?"  Or of course the never ending drone of the digger!

You had to be quick as the digger came round to the next dreel to you, ploughing the next row for you to pick up even more potatoes. The potatoes I believe were called kers pinks. The Gaffer would come along saying "c'moan hurry up stop plestering." or playing about.

You were facing the ground all the time as you were bent over in the tattie picking posture.( on all fours).

A tractor would come along; a farmhand would empty our creels on to the trailer. Like the raspberry picking there were days when you had to try to get all the potatoes or tatties that were missed on the first picking so the next stage of our work was the harrowing work (and harrowing it was). The tractor trailed a heavy frame with iron teeth. This was to drag or comb the area unearthing potatoes that the tractor had missed the first time round. This was even more back breaking as the frame was quite wide and you had a wider area to cover, and pick up the potatoes.

At the end of the day we used to walk about like half shut knives as our backs felt as if they were about to break.

Highlight of the day – you have guessed it - lunch time. The remains of the pieces we didn't eat on the way early in the morning were now eaten with hands caked in earth or mud.

We got paid the princely some of £4.00 something per week.

The transport was a tractor and trailer to work.

TATTIE PICKING I WOULD SOONER HAVE TATTIES IN MY HEELS!!

# CHAPTER TEN
## (WEDDING SCRAMBLES)

# WEDDING SCRAMBLES

Saturdays were favourite days for the bairns.
We made sure that we knew beforehand of
any wedding taking place in the town by
reading the Banns outside the post office.
This told us if there were any weddings due
to take place.
There were three popular churches for
weddings in Tayport, the Parish Church, the
Free Church, and the Church of Scotland.

**What was the attraction for us?**
The attraction was the fact that contrary to
what many sassenachs may think, Scots
actually **throw money out** to the crowds at
weddings just after the couple is married.
The best man usually has the responsibility to
do this.
The relatives were usually first out   at the
church gates to officially greet the newly
married couple, but we  always beat them to
it. We were always there first! There was
always a little group of us bairns gathered in
the prime position at the entrance so that
when money was thrown out, we were the
first in the scramble jumping and shrieking in
the air to catch some money then scrambling
on the ground to collect as much as we could.
Sometimes you could hear the coins rolling

down the street.

One wedding I remember vividly was the wedding of a really bonnie local bride, Cathy Gilmour. The wedding took place at the King St Church. Her best man must have got carried away as I think that he threw out the money from the wrong pocket and threw out his own money instead! I saw a half crown fly through the air and when it landed I put my foot on it; unfortunately it was just beside the wedding car and everyone was taking pictures of the bride and groom, but my foot stood firmly on the ground with this half crown underneath. I wouldn't budge as I did not want to lose the half crown (I had never seen this amount of money at a wedding before).

So the traditional picture taken of the bride and groom had a scruffy 12 year old girl in the foreground standing in a very odd looking position with her foot jutting out at a funny angle.

Scots *still* throw money out at weddings
WHA'S LIKE US!!!

# CHAPTER ELEVEN
## (3D WORTH OF AULDERS)

# 3D WORTH OF AULDERS

Money was scarce for most of us just after the war, in fact "as scarce as the hair on a bee's knees" some of the older folks said, so our families had to be imaginative in order to cope.

Friday nights we lived like royalty (Friday was of course pay day) so the housewives used to go to places like the Co-op or the Store as it was known. This was SCWS. On these nights, things like biscuits and gingerbread and oatcakes were tucked into. On really special nights it was perhaps white pudding supper, black pudding supper or fish and chips, washed down with American cream soda or Vimto.

By Saturday it was scraping the barrel again. Some days it was bread and milk (saps) only. Some of us went to the local 'chippie' the fish and chip shop, and asked for 3d worth of curlie wurlies. These were the little bits of batter that dropped off the battered fish or mealy puddings. You probably remember seeing them in the fish trays. You can of course still see them there but I don't think there is anyone going in to buy a portion of them! Anyway, we bought 3d worth of these which were served in a wee white poke with jagged edges.

Many mothers sold their sweetie and clothing ration coupons to some of the posh residents or 'pan-loafie' people in the town in order to pay their bills.

My father used some of this money to back on the horses. He always placed a two way bet under his nom de plume of Piper. It was a long time before I realised what an each way bet was. I always thought the horses had to run there and back to be an each- way race! We also used to collect empty lemonade bottles and take them back to the shops to get tuppence on the bottles (the youngest bairn was usually tricked in to doing this.)

What I remember most of all was going to the bakers, Grahame and Gibbs .This shop was on a brae in Whitenhill I was under strict instruction to stay outside the shop window on the brae and peer in ( this I literally did with nose pressed flat against the window until such time there were no other customers in the shop and only one person serving - that person had to be Ella McDairmid). She always filled up the bag (incidentally it was a net bag) to the very top and she would put in extras for us not only nice tea bread like Paris buns and Pavement stones, but a few nice cakes as well.

My brothers Maurice and Stewart waited at

the top of the brae to grab the best scones.
Ella  McDairmid was very kind to us.
YES WE HAD TO USE OUR LOAF

# CHAPTER TWELVE
## (THE PICTURES OR THE FLICKS)

# THE PICTURES OR FLICKS

Going to the Saturday matinee was a favourite pastime for the bairns (the bigger bairns too).
I believe it was 7d to get in.
The serial that drew most attention was Flash Gordon. This was a very exciting programme. We really lived this.
The Bowery boys were another favourite.
Satch the glaikit one who was the first person I knew to wear the baseball cap back to front!
Mugsy Mahone who wore a wide brimmed hat and a smile to match - the clever dick!
Louie Dombrouski the short round shopkeeper.

Geronimo was yet another favourite The boys of the town frequently calling out *Geronimo very loudly* as they went running passed unsuspecting pedestrians.
They used to like to call each other Big Chief of the Black Feet
One Picture that we managed to see was The Beast with Five Fingers. We got in to see this with an 'adult', usually a bigger bairn pretending to be older.

The story of the Beast as far as I can

remember was about a pianist who had his hand damaged and some deranged doctor grafted on the hand of a dead person. The bit was that the hand was from a deranged strangler and when it was grafted on to the pianist, he started murdering innocent people as he had no control over this hand. Eventually the hand was cut off but alas the hand now had a life of its own and the hand itself would strangle people. In the final scene the hand is playing the piano on its own then - IT SUDDENLY STRANGLES THE PIANIST HIMSELF WHO APPEARS ON THE SCENE.

We were absolutely terrified and rooted to our seats.

In 1951/52 there was great excitement everyone was talking about 3D pictures coming to town.

Well the upshot was that we went to the cinema and were given special glasses to wear. We had to hold them up to our eyes in order to see these fantastic effects.

Everyone was screaming INCLUDING THE ADULTS. The talk had gone round the town beforehand that it could be dangerous "You could lose your sight if you don't wear the glasses" they said.

The film was the most amazing film I have ever seen. It showed to its greatest advantage

# <u>WHEESHT!</u>

reptiles as if they were slithering out to get you, tigers that appeared to walk down the aisle, a ladder that came out and appeared to hit you on your head. The audience was screeching. The usherettes, I think, gave up trying to shoosh us as the adults were just as bad if not worse. What a night!!!

There has never been anything like it before or after.

Our picture house in Tayport was run by the J.B. Milne group of cinemas. I think the Gaumont and the Greens Playhouse in Dundee were run by that group as well.

Many nights it was standing room only as we stood down the aisles to see the favourite films.

The first three rows in the front were extremely uncomfortable, very hard and painted a very dark brown. They were the cheap seats, mainly used by the bairns, and known as the scratchers. It cost 9d to get in. The posh soft seats were the 1/9's; also there was a 'balcony', a slightly raised section that went up in height gradually to the giddy height of about 2ft!

We, of course, always sat in the scratchers . One local woman who seemed to go to see every film was nicknamed by us as Mrs TUT TUT because she always sat in the first or second row of the soft seats,   right in the middle of the row and tutted and tutted all night long about our behaviour. Another regular picture goer only appeared to have one tooth. We reckoned she kept that for cracking nuts!!

The Picture House was a very popular place indeed, the films changed three times a week.
Mon Tues -Wed Thurs - Fri Sat.
There were so many cowboy films shown there that according to Mrs Homer the Manageress they thought of calling it the ranch.
Roy Rogers and Trigger - Wild Bill Hickock - Gabby Hayes etc., were some of the characters I remember best.
We always had a sweetie to eat - frequently (because it was the cheapest ) we had a ha'penny stick of black liquorice, pretty ghastly, or maybe some soor plooms or granny sookers to sook or suck during the film.
It was a sad day when the picture house closed down.
We took it for granted.
YOU DINNAE MISS THE WATER 'TIL THE WELL RUNS DRY.

# CHAPTER THIRTEEN
## (PLEASE COULD YOU HELP THE GUISERS?)

## PLEASE COULD YOU HELP THE GUISERS?

A few weeks before Halloween was another very exciting time for us as this was when we dressed up in whatever 'claes' or clothes we could find or get a hold of, to go round 'chappin' on the doors and saying "please could you help the guisers?" Some of us were dressed up as sweepies with our faces blackened and old cloth bonnets on our heads. I went one year as Ingin Johnnie *
I had a long string tied round my neck. This would be as long as a scarf reaching from one hand round the neck to the other hand and one large onion or ( ingin) tied at either end. Some people gave us a penny or a threepenny bit each. We had to put on a performance like singing or dancing, before some people would part with their money.
I used to sing Ye Banks and Braes. Most people gave me the money before I finished the first verse. Whether it was the awful singing or the smell of the onions (probably rotting by this time) that brought it to a sudden end, I will never know.
Miss Wills reportedly of the Woodbine Cigarette family lived in Grey St., She was very generous and gave everybody sixpence or a 'tanner'. Word went round like wild fire and she was everyone's first port of call.

We dressed up as something different the next night and called again for another sixpence. If she knew it was us again she never let on!

This was the build up to Halloween.

* Ingin Johnnies

Spaniards used to come over from Dundee on the Fifie * with their bikes and they had long strings of Onion ( Ingins  ) round their neck. The string was long and used to rest on the handlebars of their bikes. They cycled round the streets selling their onions on very wobbly bikes they were a very familiar sight.

- Fifie -The Ferry from Dundee to Newport
- Ingins- Onions
- Sweepie -The coal sweep
- Guisers - children dressed up as someone else (disguised)

# CHAPTER FOURTEEN
## (DOOKIN FOR APPLES)

# 'DOOKIN' FOR APPLES

This was supposed to be an evening for the bairns - what a hope!

This usually turned out to be a night the bairns decided who was their MER (most embarrassing relative ).

Picture the scene - Halloween in a neighbour's house, bairns outnumbered by about 4 to 1, a big tin bath with apples floating in it. (The apples were more often than not cooking apples or apples a bit past their best).

We had to bend over the bath with a fork in our mouth, the handle held in place by our teeth then 'dook' for apples, that is to try to secure an apple by plunging your head in to the bath.

The adults took sheer delight in pushing our heads in even further and us getting soaking wet!!

The prize of course was getting one of the apples. We were horrified when after securing an apple we sunk our teeth in only to find a maggot, but were mortified when we bit in to the apple and found half a maggot and wondered where the other half had gone!

We were soon pushed out of the way as the adults got carried away trying to do these themselves. They were often lying on the floor kicking their feet in hysterical laughter at each other, shouting between guffaws "your turn next Jock or Wullie". While this was going on the bairns would look down their noses at them disowning them. Unfortunately in these small towns everybody seemed to be related.

There, more often than not, would be a wee man sitting on a chair in the corner with a woodbine doupie (cigarette end ) hanging out the corner of his mouth, moaning and groaning about all thae (these) idiots making fools of themselves.

Someone would always take the floor and sing:-

"I'm the saftest o' the faimely". The chorus went something like this...................

I'm the saftest o' the faimely !
I'm the simple Johnnie Raw!
For ev-er-y thing my mither blames me,
And ma faither puts it on me an a'.

That started everybody off. They all wanted to sing, including the wee man who up until now would have nothing to do with the 'singing'.

So what happened was that everybody sang their own song (all different) at the same time. There wasn't a lot of room when they all stood up. What with trying to avoid the

long flypaper that was hanging down from
the pulley (the flypaper was probably about
18 inches long) and trying not to stand on
each others feet, what a carry on!

Most popular songs were

Will ye stop yer tic-kle-ing Jock
Stop yer tic-kle-ing tic-kle-ic-kle ickle-ing
Stop yer tickleing jock
- I'm no awa tae bide awa I'm no awa to
lave ye
- A wee deoch and Doris
The cue for us to go home was when your
mother got up to sing with throat warbling
and eyelids flickering and giving a rendition
of the Road and the Miles tae
Dundee..............

# CHAPTER FIFTEEN
## (DO YOU REMEMBER)

# Do You Remember?

## Ringlets

Having your hair tied up at night with long strips of cloth, like bandages tied round your hair to make your hair fall down in ringlets. There was a variation of the ringlet this was when the ringlet itself with the cloth in place was wound round like a little knot so that in place of ringlets in the morning your hair was bouncy with curls. This was known as having jumpers in your hair. I could only imagine they were called that because in the morning your hair jumped out in ridiculous curls.

## Clootie Rugs

Some women made fireside rugs from 'auld cloots' or rags. My Auntie Tam (Thomasina Ferrier) made beautiful rugs which were very thick and colourful and lasted for years. Some are still in use today.

## End of Term

The entire school milling out to attend church at the end of term, before breaking up for 7 x weeks of summer holidays.
Everyone bellowed out the following hymn;
Summer suns are glowing over land and sea happy light is flowing bountiful and free

everywhere resounding in the mellow rays all earth's thousand voices sing a song of praise.

This made us all think of a happy peaceful world. (Not here yet)!

I'll keep in mind the words of Robert Burns particularly the last verse of my mother's favourite poem;-

A Man's a Man for a, that

Then let us pray that come it may
As come it will for a' that,
That Sense and Worth o'er a' the earth,
Shall bear the gree an a' that.
For a' that an a' that,
It's coming yet for a' that, That man to man,
the world o'er Shall brithers be for a' that.

### Message Boys

Some shops, frequently bakers, grocers or fruit and vegetable shops, employed  people, usually young boys, to deliver their food namely their messages on bicycles to householders. These bikes were a great boon as very few people had cars at that time. The bikes had a very big basket at the front - a very familiar sight.

## Gas Man  and Money Back

What joy when we were told by our friends
that the gas man was doing his rounds? Our
gas man was in fact Mr Blaikie, a very kind
person who came round a few times each
year to empty the meter. It took him several
days to cover Tayport so we kept track of the
streets that he was working; there was a daily
update as to how near he was to getting to our
house. The reason for such interest was that
there was always money back.

The meter took pennies or shillings; usually it
was pennies that we had in the meter as it
was difficult to part with a shilling in one go.
(12 x old pennies)

These pennies were over an inch wide so the
pile of these large pennies that were returned
to us seemed an awful lot of money.

The adults and children really looked forward
to these occasions.

## Sloans of Dundee

Shop, where most of us bought our clothes
and household goods.  G.L. Wilson's , D.M.
Brown's and Draffens were the  most widely
known shops.

## Co-op Divi (Dividend)

The local Co-op paid out a dividend to their
members periodically. This was like a loyalty

bonus. Every time we bought the weekly messages that is to say food shopping we gave them our number, our number was 1054.

## Special Orange Juice
Lovely thick orange juice in what looked like a medicine bottle; I believe this was supplied by the school clinic, a wonderful taste.

## Extract of Malt and All That
We were plied with things like Extract of Malt, Syrup of Figs and Andrews Liver Salts in order to make us strong!
On one occasion at the baby school when we were about 5 or 6 we were given a paper poke (bag) with a chocolate powder and sugar crystals in it to make drinks from. This was to be taken home; I think this was also some sort of medicine to build us up. I thought it was sherbet dab and dipped my fingers in it until it was finished it never reached home.

## Christening Piece
When babies were christened in the Church it was customary in some areas to hand out a Christening Piece. When a baby boy was christened the Parents or Godparents handed out a little bag to the first girl or woman that

they met (I am not sure if this was on the way to the church or on the way back). The bag contained things like a piece of the Christening cake and a 'lucky penny'. If it was a baby girl that was being Christened then this was handed out to the first boy that they met. It was considered a great privilege to receive a Christening piece.

## Stop Me and Buy One  Bikes

Pedal or Push Bikes, with a section in front; that contained ice cream where you could buy a slider or a cone. This was like a three wheeler bike with one wheel at the back and a sort of square tub on the front with two wheels.  These bikes were always there at sports days, football matches, and highland games etc., Angus Barbeiri used to pedal this bike to all these events.

## School Sports Day
This was planned with great precision. The teachers turning in to sport coaches.
Parents made a special effort to be there.
Mine were forbidden (by me)
One day as I was at the starter line kneeling on one knee waiting to run at the sound of the gun going off.  I heard  a voice in the crowd

' c'moan Vera '. My Auntie Agg (Agnes Cavanagh) was there in the crowd so when the gun went off I ran extremely fast - faster than I had ever run before but the opposite way! Too embarrassed to run in front of my Auntie! This put the whole team in to utter confusion and the race was declared null and void.

## Clay Pipes for Soapy Bubbles

We bought real clay pipes from the tobacconist in our case these were bought from Scott's in Broad St., We used these pipes to blow soapy bubbles from.

## Swapping Scraps

Buying and swapping scraps. Paper pictures kept between the pages of a book and swapping these pictures between our friends whilst sitting in the playground shelter (do you remember the little angels' just their heads with either pink or blue wings?)

## Catching tadpoles

Catching tadpoles and bringing them home in a jam jar. (No-one told me that they turned in to frogs!)

## Cam

I have never seen this word written so I hope the spelling is acceptable. This is a stone that was used after washing the doorstep to make the steps look clean and smart. When the stone was wet, housewives used to go round the edges of the stairs or steps rubbing this stone in circular movements to give a nice white or cream border.

## Rolling your Egg

We used to have hard, really extremely hard boiled eggs to roll at Easter time this was to signify the Stone being rolled away from Christ's grave. We hand painted these eggs, using our own design. We went on a picnic, then from a hill or slope rolled the egg down the hill time and time again until it cracked. The harder the egg the longer it lasted without breaking of course. We had a sort of competition to see whose egg lasted the longest.

## Stone Hot Water Bottles

Very heavy and hard stone hot water bottles. They were stone or beige in colour and had a little knob at one end. The knob to fill the bottle was on the side.

This was put in the middle of the bed and as it was quite round it lifted the bedcovers up slightly so the heat spread from there.

## Cummies or Accumulators

These were charged up nearly every week as they were the power to make the wireless or radio work.

Little square, longish bottles, containing some type of acid. When they needed charging it was said they need more juice. They had to be charged up for Saturday afternoon for the football results. Very often we had to sit silently and not breathe too loud so that our parents could literally have their ears to the wireless to hear.

## Pom Poms

Making pom poms using two milk bottle tops from the little bottles of milk that we got daily at school

## Rag and Bone Man

The rag and bone man used to call regularly to collect rags. Many a skelp (smack) I had because if I saw him on the way home I would go round the corner and take off my jumper and hand it to the Rag and Bone man in exchange for a threepenny bit.

## Spot the Odd One Out

Shopkeepers in town put something in their window that didn't belong to their type of shop. It was very difficult to spot the odd one out as sometimes it was very subtle. For example, a bakers shop would have something like a box of chocolates keeking or (peeping) out from under a cake stand.

We had to go round all the shops and list the item that was out of place or the odd one out. We stared in the windows for hours looking for the answer. We called over the street to other groups who were looking in the shop windows thinking they would share their answers - what a hope!

The shopkeepers really benefited from the interest shown in their shops.

## Forfeits

Favourite party game usually played by the adults at a children's party.

This game had numerous variations. The one we used was with little bits of paper with writing on thrown like confetti on to the floor.

The most ridiculous things were written on it. The recipient of this paper was to perform some of these ridiculous tasks. I remember arriving late to a party and was greeted by my mother at the doorstep in Ogilvy Place with her screeching over and over again at the top of her voice " I'm my mother's big bubbly bair-inn" (bairn). I hid under a bush until my friends passed before going in to the party.

## Miscellaneous

- Using slates and pencils at school instead of paper and pencil-
- Half loaf, or loaf and a half. - Buying bread in half loafs or multiples of halves.
- Grannies on the chimneys - Little hats as it were, that birled in the wind dissipating the smoke.
- Tackets - Little tackets or tacks in the soles of your shoes to make them last longer.  We loved these because if you ran and skidded on the pavement the tackets used to make sparks.
- Getting the Smit - Catching a disease from someone else.
- Shaky Doon - A make shift bed when staying the night somewhere unexpectedly.
- Galluses - Trouser Braces.
- Crafty Coin Toss - Heads I win Tails you lose.
- Moonlichtie - Moonlight Flit. Moving house over night deliberately so that no one would know where you went.
- Face as long as Lieth Walk. - Someone with a miserable look on their face

# POEM BY MAURICE MILNE

A day begins ……………..what lies ahead?


A day begins what lies ahead
Simple things or events to dread
As it enfolds we change to cope
To find a way to renew hope
To consider others not use as a tool
To exercise wisdom not act like a fool
Looking back on the day as it draws to a close
Regretting some actions that's how life goes


MAURICE MILNE

1932 – 1998

**All that glitters is not gold**

*All gold does not glitter!*

*Some have gold but do not recognise it.*

The Abercraig (Fifie)
Leaving Newport for Dundee © D.C. Thomson & Co., Ltd

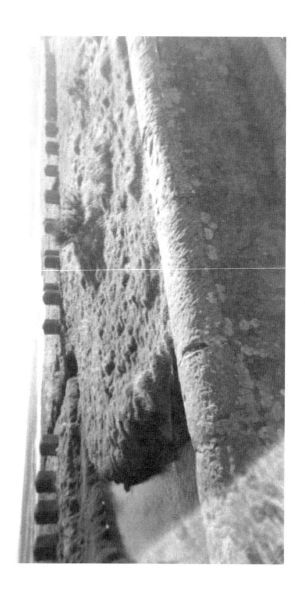

Tay Estuary showing Anti Tank defence pillars

Royal Yacht Britannia sails down the Tay in 1955
© D.C. Thomson & Co., Ltd

A.S.R. Boat Hanger Tayport
Courtesy RAF Museum Hendon

Tayport Harbour. Late 1940's. Air Sea Rescue Launch
Billets & Harbour Master's Office. Courtesy RAF Museum Hendon

Inside Boat Hanger Tayport
Courtesy RAF Museum Hendon

Inside A.S.R. Billets Tayport
Courtesy RAF Museum Hendon

Steam Train passing the Old Harbour Tayport
© Copyright Alistair F Nisbet

The Campania in Dundee
Festival of Britain 1951 © D.C. Thomson & Co., Ltd

Fresh Fruit & Veg Delivery by Wullie Doctor
Courtesy of Andrew Phin

Ration Book